VISIONARY PATH
TAROT
A 78-CARD DECK

LUCY DELICS

Park Street Press
Rochester, Vermont

Park Street Press
One Park Street
Rochester, Vermont 05767
www.ParkStPress.com

Park Street Press is a division of Inner Traditions International

ISBN 978-1-64411-060-7

Printed and bound in China by Reliance Printing Co., Ltd.

10 9 8 7 6 5 4 3 2 1

Text design and layout by Priscilla Baker
This book was typeset in Garamond Premier Pro with Nexa
and Gill Sans used as display typefaces

To send correspondence to the author of this book, mail a
first-class letter to the author c/o Inner Traditions • Bear &
Company, One Park Street, Rochester, VT 05767, and we will
forward the communication, or contact the author directly at
www.thedelics.org.

I heard a calling from deep within,
Since my lungs first learned to sing,
I followed its sound to the depth of my soul,
Where I found the light that guided me home.

Introduction

The story of the *Visionary Path Tarot* began when I arrived in the Sacred Valley of the Incas in the Andean region of Peru. I didn't know what was waiting for me here, but as my plane landed in Cusco, I felt like I had arrived home—a feeling I had forgotten over the years of nomadic living.

I had been dreaming about Peru since childhood. When I was young my fascination was focused on the magical ancient history, but as I got older and had my first psychedelic experiences it became about the sacred plants that heal through inducing visionary states. This was why I eventually came to this beautiful place.

My father died when I was just fifteen; then a couple of years later my mother was diagnosed with lung cancer. Just after my twentieth birthday I became an orphan—alone, scared, and lost. As a child I had many dreams filled with magic and adventure, but now survival mode set in. I don't believe the society I grew up in did its best to encourage my creativity; in fact, by the time I left school I had forgotten that I had any artistic talent, and I had given up on creative outlets. I tried to cling to my dreams of adventure; so a year to the day after my mother passed was my first day at university studying archaeology. I got my degree, but during those three years it became very evident that I was not going to discover the meaning of life in academia.

Instead of attending my graduation, I was at the Palestinian West Bank trying to teach teenagers about heritage protection during conflict. As I looked out across the landscape, divided, with a stench of fear, my outlook on life became very bleak. I spent some time hanging around the holy sites of Jerusalem, and while I was people watching I caught a glimpse of a nun's eyes as she sat in the corner of the Church of the Holy Sepulchre. There was not the desperation in her eyes that I saw in the masses of pilgrims taking selfies as they got blessed by unimpressed priests. In her eyes was peace—something that I was seeking. I had no interest in following an Abrahamic path; my spirit had always been too pagan for that. But she was on a path. I wanted to be on a path, too—a path of seeking, of knowledge, of peace, and, most importantly, a path of love.

I had not planned ahead; after university I had no money, no home to go back to, and a hangover from all the alcohol with which the system likes to fill young people. I arrived back in Coventry, the English city where I grew up. I was on the dole and sleeping on a friend's sofa. As much as I had and still have love for the place that raised me, an unconscious part of me was seeking nature instead of concrete. I applied for housekeeping jobs where they provided food and accommodation, and a few days later I found myself on the Highland Express. I had gotten a job in Scotland, the land of my mother's people. The wildness of this place overwhelmed me; the Celtic tongue and music resonated with something deep within, and the peace and tranquillity found within the landscape allowed me to begin the long work of healing the septic grief I had been carrying.

My next stop was the Arctic Circle; during the winter season I found myself working in a hotel at the very north of Sweden, bordering Finland. I didn't see the sun for more than two and a half months. My work colleagues and I were all going through emotional processes due to this. Then one day, like a divine God, it returned—the Sun. We could do nothing but feel grateful and stare in awe. I was also able to experience the Northern Lights, one of the best displays in fifteen years, a local said. The green lights then turned pink and yellow and danced above me. How could this be a natural phenomenon? It was so magical to behold! More healing was granted to me here, but I still had a long way to go. The landscapes of northwestern Europe also spoke to ancestral memories inside. I cannot say for sure, but due to my father's looks and the part of England and Scotland from which his family came, a place heavily settled by Vikings, I had always felt some northern songs singing in my ancestral soundtrack. I wanted to connect to this more and found myself a volunteer opportunity as a Viking.

Gudvangen, the Viking Valley—I cannot express to you how much this place gave me, how much magic was restored to my being while I meditated alone in the fjords. The nature is so loud there; it's almost shouting. I started to remember the magic, to remember the light within. Although dim, I could see it now. I spent the entire summer of 2011 barefoot in a linen dress, covered by a reindeer hide, living inside a tent with Viking knot work carved into the wooden frame. I made important friends who became a loving family. People believed in me. After my mum died, for a long time I blamed myself; I never liked the conventional treatment she got for her illness—the morphine, the chemo . . . All this destroyed her quality of life, and she died with fear. I had hated myself ever since, until here, until people showed me that I was worthy of love again. My magic was back with me, and I was on a path that felt very clearly like my path now. In Gudvangen, I also started to communicate with nature, particularly trees, in some unspoken language from eons ago.

My next spot was working in a small bed-and-breakfast in the English Lake District. I arrived for my interview and on the same day got the job; so to celebrate I visited a local stone circle known as Castlerigg. I gave an offering of a silver triskel pendant and buried it in the middle of this site. As I gave thanks to Spirit for helping me get here, I asked for protection and support on the path: a path that was still much unknown to me. The small old coach house where I lived was the place where William Wordsworth's son once kept his horses, and the bed-and-breakfast was once the Wordsworth residence. I could feel the inspiration in the air. The beauty of my surroundings comforted my spirit and encouraged me to explore. I immediately fell in love with this place. I started to go on hikes for the first time. I would spend days up the fells meditating and exploring. I made more tree friends; I found trails up the mountains where tourists wouldn't go, granting me space to explore the nature around me alone, wild, and free. Poetry started to come, like it did when I was younger, and some sketches started to fill the pages of notebooks during my adventures around this ancient land.

It was 2012, a year I had always had an interest in ever since I heard about the Mayan Calendar as a girl during my Indiana Jones–Lara Croft dream years. I never believed in some horrifying end of the world doomsday for which this date became known, I always felt it was just a marking in time of a new time, like a new Yuga for humanity.

I was finally starting to process the pain of losing my mother. I had found peace with my father's death, although still hard, but for years my mother's death had been too painful to even think about. I started to explore the healing plants of this world while I was learning about alternative ways of healing sickness. I became obsessed with the psychedelic experience and how it could have given my mother peace of mind and acceptance of death. Although I had a few beautiful experiences with LSD in previous years, they were largely recreational. Now I felt like I was discovering the missing link. I started to gather the magic mushrooms, which grew all around this region, during the most pagan time of year. I also started to journey with magical truffles, alone in a dark room. I had some of the most profound experiences of my life. My intention wasn't recreational anymore, but healing, magical, and therapeutic. This felt so archaic, like I was following the shamanic path of the ancients, remembering the plants and fungi, remembering the traditions of how humanity experienced mind-altering states in dark caves long ago. I planned at the end of the year to finally visit Peru, mainly the Amazon rain forest, in search of ayahuasca. I thought I was seeking something, but in truth it was seeking me.

And then there I was; it all felt effortless, like some Force was bringing me to the jungle. I was scared, about to drink, and my ego wanted to run away. However, my heart wanted to stay. The first time I stayed for five weeks in the jungle, drinking ayahuasca and huachuma. It was not easy at first to let go, to get over myself. Once I did, the magical transformation began. Spirit doctors healed my heart; I felt the love for all things inside, emanating from my being like a light. I had a vision of the divine, a spinning disco ball in the highest reaches of the cosmic attic. It projected holographic material into the darkness of matter, and it was into this projector that everything returned. I shape-shifted into a large cat and felt a freedom unknown to human comprehension. A divine comedy, the system, the slavery of the machine I grew up in—I laughed it off, became free, and returned to my heart. It was my heart, the navigation device; the heart came first, the mind second. It felt wonderful to remember something so important. In the nights of visionary experience, seeing music, hearing color, I remembered my ultimate truth: I was an artist . . . how did I ever forget?

After all this magic I tried to go back—back to the Western world. I couldn't stay. As the reality set in that I was an artist, I decided to stop cleaning people's holiday messes in hotels. I stopped giving my energy to a system that didn't serve me. I knew I had to return to the land that freed me; I still had something to complete there. As I arrived in the Sacred Valley of Peru, I knew I had a task, a magic initiation to fulfill . . . the tarot. Channeled from high up in the Andes, this is my gift to you to help you remember that your dreams are just as real as mine. We can all dwell in the heart and manifest the life we dreamed of as a child. We are all free. I didn't know anyone as I started this creation, and now as I write this I sit next to my beautiful family as a loving partner and mother.

My wish is for this tarot deck to assist you on your path of discovering your true purpose. I hope it can bring you peace and inspiration and help shed some insights and clues for you and for the person who is being read.

And remember, most importantly, love—love before and beyond everything else.

Urpijay Sonqoy
(A dove from my heart, Quechuan
metaphor for "Thank you!")

The Major Arcana

The Fool
Upright: Free Spirit, Adventure, Innocence, Exploration
Reversed: Naïveté, Inconsideration, Recklessness

The Magician
Upright: Creation, Magic, Craft, Alchemy, Visions
Reversed: Illusions, Trickery, Sorcery, Ego

The High Priestess
Upright: Medicine Woman, Inner Voice, Intuition, Divine
    Feminine, Creativity
Reversed: Lost Intuition, Lack of Belief, Repressed Emotions,
    Lack of Expression

The Empress
Upright: Motherhood, Sacred Feminine, Fertility, Nature
Reversed: Smothering, Self-Loathing, Dependence

The Emperor
Upright: Authority, Fatherhood, Sacred Masculine, Leadership
Reversed: Lack of Emotions, Rigidity, Tyranny

The Hierophant
Upright: Morality, Ethics, Tradition, Knowledge
Reversed: Anarchy, Chaos, Rebellion

The Lovers
Upright: Partnership, Union, Sacred Family, Duality, Mirror
Reversed: Disharmony, Lost Meaning, Selfishness, Imbalance

The Chariot
Upright: Willpower, Control, Direction and Vision
Reversed: Aggression, Anger, Lost Path

Justice
Upright: Truth, Karma, Clarity, Faith
Reversed: Corruption, Dishonesty, Lack of Morals

The Hermit
Upright: Sacred, Creativity, Channeling, Inner Strength,
   Reflection and Contemplation
Reversed: Isolation, Lost, Scared, Uncontrollable Feelings of
   Loneliness

The Wheel of Fortune
Upright: Fate, Cycles, Change
Reversed: Bad Luck, Negative Influence, Trying to Control

Strength
Upright: Brave Heart, Compassion, Strength Inner and Outer, Focus and Dedication
Reversed: Defeat, Self-Doubt, Weakness and Self-Loathing

The Hanged Man
Upright: Martyrdom, Sacrifice, Surrender
Reversed: Selfishness, Inflated Ego, Unforgiving

Death
Upright: Beginnings, Metamorphosis, Adventure, Birth
Reversed: Stagnant Waters, Decay, Materialism, Holding On

Temperance
Upright: Patience, Meaning, Enlightenment, Path with Heart, Manifestation
Reversed: Unbalanced Emotions, Excess and Extremes

The Devil
Upright: Materialism, Addictive Tendencies, Lust
Reversed: Letting Go, Balance, Freedom

The Tower
Upright: Something to Overcome, Disaster, Danger Ahead, Shock
Reversed: Danger Avoided (for now), Fear of Unknown and Suffering

The Star
Upright: Rebirth, Light, Faith, Hope
Reversed: Insecurity, Lack of Belief, God-Fearing

The Moon
Upright: Dreams, Intuition, Illusions
Reversed: Control, Manipulation, Misguided Power, Lack of
    Clarity

The Sun
Upright: Illumination, Salvation, Success, Happiness, Positive
    Vibrations
Reversed: Low Frequencies, Negative Outlook, Lost and
    Self-Loathing

Judgment
Upright: Awakening, Inner Reflection, Balance
Reversed: Projections, Fear, Lack of Confidence, Confines of
    Mind

The World
Upright: Peace, Harmony, Material, Conclusion
Reversed: Unresolved Work to Do, Ego Struggles

The Minor Arcana

CUPS

Ace of Cups
Upright: New Love, Compassion, Creativity, Understanding
Reversed: Vanity, Repressed Expression

2 of Cups
Upright: Partnership, Love, Mutual Attraction
Reversed: Distrust, Breakups, Egotism

3 of Cups
Upright: Friendship, Community, Celebration, Artistic Expression
Reversed: Space, Independence, Reflection, Recuperation

4 of Cups
Upright: Meditation, Enlightenment, Epiphany, Reflection
Reversed: Withdrawal, Retreat, Time Out

5 of Cups
Upright: Pessimism, Regret, Failure, Negativity
Reversed: Self-Love, Forgiveness, Evolution

6 of Cups
Upright: Memories, Childhood, Spirit, Happiness, Innocence
Reversed: Stiff Body Language, Lack of Play, Living in the Past

7 of Cups
Upright: Wishful Thinking, Illusions, Decisions, Opportunity
Reversed: Overwhelmed, Negative Thought Patterns

8 of Cups
Upright: Escapism, Withdrawal, Disappointment, Abandonment
Reversed: Drifting, Walking Away, Directionless

9 of Cups
Upright: Wish Granted, Contentment, Satisfaction, Gratitude
Reversed: Indulgence, Materialism, Dissatisfaction

10 of Cups
Upright: Divinity, Love, Connection, Soul Mate, Bliss, Positive Frequency
Reversed: Relationship Struggles, Misalignment, Disconnection

Queen of Cups
Upright: Intuition, Sacred Feminine, Motherhood, Caring, Compassion
Reversed: Codependency, Self-Love, Inner Feelings

King of Cups
Upright: Diplomatic, Justice, Balance
Reversed: Manipulative, Suppressed Emotions, Unbalanced, Moodiness

Knight of Cups
Upright: Creativity, Charm, Vision, Imagination, Dreams, Romance
Reversed: Manipulative, Controlling, Jealously

Page of Cups
Upright: Intuition, Creative Opportunities, Curiosity, Possibilities
Reversed: Immature, Creative Block, Self-Doubt

SWORDS

Ace of Swords
Upright: Clarity, Breakthrough, Victory, Glory
Reversed: Lack of Clarity, Chaos, Defeat

2 of Swords
Upright: Blindness, Blocked Emotions, Truce, Choices
Reversed: Confusion, Overthinking, Indecision

3 of Swords
Upright: Heartbreak, Grief, Sorrow, Rejection
Reversed: Forgiveness, Compassion, Letting Go, Moving On

4 of Swords
Upright: Rest, Rejuvenation, Contemplation, Relaxation
Reversed: Overworked, Lack of Rest or Relaxation

5 of Swords
Upright: Resentment, Defeat, Conflict, Betrayal, Loss
Reversed: Openness, Forgiveness, Peace

6 of Swords
Upright: Ceremony, Initiation, Necessary Transition
Reversed: Unfinished Business, Holding On, Fear

7 of Swords
Upright: Untrustworthy, Immoral Behavior, Betrayal, Strategy
Reversed: Breaking Behavior Patterns, Caught Out, Shame

8 of Swords
Upright: Indoctrination, Limitation, Closed-Mindedness
Reversed: Acceptance, Freedom, Evolution

9 of Swords
Upright: Anxiety, Nightmares, Low Vibrations, Worry
Reversed: Perspective, Relaxation, Patience, Understanding

10 of Swords
Upright: Betrayal, Endings, Negative Influence
Reversed: Rebirth, Lessons, New Avenue, Light Ahead

Queen of Swords
Upright: Independence, Freedom, Organization,
   Intelligence
Reversed: Coldness, No Compassion, Unkindness

King of Swords
Upright: Truth, Authority, Power, Rational Thinking
Reversed: Abusive, Tyrannical, Dictating

Knight of Swords
Upright: Intense, Hasty, Opinionated, Active
Reversed: Unclear Thinking, Secretive

Page of Swords
Upright: Curious, Energetic, Restless, Egotistic
Reversed: Pipe Dreamer

PENTACLES

Ace of Pentacles
Upright: Abundance, Opportunity, Ideas, Reception
Reversed: No Foresight, Missed Opportunity

2 of Pentacles
Upright: Balance, Adaptability, Organization
Reversed: Imbalance, Financial Difficulties, Disorganization

3 of Pentacles
Upright: Knowledge, Teamwork, Collaboration, Positivity
Reversed: Selfish, Disrespectful, Negative Emotions

4 of Pentacles
Upright: Security, Stability, Ownership, Control
Reversed: Self-Protection, Ecologically Minded, Unstable Behavior

5 of Pentacles
Upright: Poverty, Worry, Stress, Isolation
Reversed: Spiritual Depletion, Recovery

6 of Pentacles
Upright: Sharing, Charity, Kindness, Giving, Prosperity
Reversed: Selfishness, Debt, Decay

7 of Pentacles
Upright: Investment, Vision, Positive Outlook, Hard
   Work, Reward
Reversed: Limitation, Illusions, Fleeting Reward

8 of Pentacles
Upright: Apprenticeship, Education, Engagement,
   Communication, Expansion
Reversed: Unfocused, Perfectionism, Closed to
   New Ideas

9 of Pentacles
Upright: Independence, Freedom, Comfort, Gratitude, Culmination
Reversed: Workaholic, Financial Struggle, Bad Health

10 of Pentacles
Upright: Destiny, Family, Wealth, Inheritance, Abundance, Retirement
Reversed: Loss, Financial Dismay, Stress

Queen of Pentacles
Upright: Motherly, Strong, Earth, Protection, Sensible, Warmth, Security
Reversed: Alone, Weak, Imbalanced Relations with Friends and Family

King of Pentacles
Upright: Discipline, Control, Rule, Power, Security
Reversed: Controlling, Domineering, Uncompassionate

Knight of Pentacles
Upright: Conventional, Mainstream, Methodical, Routine
Reversed: Bored, Stuck, Lazy, Unbroken Patterns

Page of Pentacles
Upright: Manifestation, New Vision, Patience, Hope
Reversed: Lack of Planning, Unfocused, Shortsighted

WANDS

Ace of Wands
Upright: Creativity, Manifestation, Potential, Power
Reversed: Heavy Energy, Uninspired, Creative Block

2 of Wands
Upright: Evolution, Progress, Dreams, Planning
Reversed: Devolution, Lack of Planning, Fear of the Unknown

3 of Wands
Upright: Vision, Preparation, Intuition, Trust, Expansion
Reversed: Obstacles to Dreams, Delays, Misplaced Trust

4 of Wands
Upright: Celebration, Peace, Balance, Family, Home, Community
Reversed: Transition, Longing, Lack of Communication

5 of Wands
Upright: Tension, Aggression, Conflict, Competition, Suffering
Reversed: Acceptance, Diversity, Communication

6 of Wands
Upright: Victory, Acknowledgment, Self-Belief, Transmutation
Reversed: Behavior Patterns, Egotism, Fall from Grace, Corruption

7 of Wands
Upright: Challenges, Perseverance, Not Giving Up, Competitive
Reversed: Overwhelmed, Giving Up, Lack of Willpower

8 of Wands
Upright: Travel, Movement, Change
Reversed: Frustration, Delays, Stalling

9 of Wands
Upright: Resilience, Courage, Bravery, Faith
Reversed: Paranoid, Defensive

10 of Wands
Upright: Strength, Burden, Labor, Achievement
Reversed: Carrying too Much, Avoiding Life, Not Present

Queen of Wands
Upright: Vibrancy, Inspirational, Focused, Ambitious, Motherly
Reversed: Vanity, Aggression, Bossy

King of Wands
Upright: Honor, Leadership, Respect, Vision
Reversed: Lust, Impatient, High Expectations

Knight of Wands
Upright: Adventure, Action, Charm, Energy
Reversed: Frustration, Impatient, Lazy

Page of Wands
Upright: Free Spirit, Discovery, Exploration, Open-Minded
Reversed: Pessimism, Unadventurous, Pipe Dreamer

Tarot Spreads

It is my wish that your intuition guide you to discover which spread works for you. I personally like to use the tarot and other divination cards by picking one in the morning and diving deep into what the card's meaning is reflecting in my current life situation. Sometimes I also like to draw a card before a ceremony or a hike into nature and see what the journey has in store on a spiritual level.

THE THREE-CARD SPREAD

This is a very popular traditional tarot spread and is quite efficient at getting answers fast. It is unique in that there is not one fixed goal to be understood and is perfect for questions and is read by understanding the context of the first card, the focus of the second, and the outcome of the third. For example:

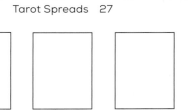

Past	Present	Future
Mind	Body	Spirit
You	Your Family	Your Relationships

The Three-Card Spread

THE FIVE-CARD SPREAD

The five-card spread (shown on page 28) is a deeper journey into the tarot and can offer up more information on the problem or question.

In this spread the cards form a cross. The card in the center represents the current situation, the card on the right is about future outcomes, and the card on the left shows us the past that is still influencing the present. The bottom card represents the reasons behind current events, and the card on top represents the different outcomes when moving forward.

Different
outcomes
when
moving
forward

Past that
is still
influencing
the present

Current
situation

Future
outcomes

Reasons
behind
current
events

The Five-Card Spread

THE CELTIC CROSS SPREAD

This spread uses ten cards: card 1 is placed in the center, card 2 on the top, turned to the side to form a cross, 5 above 1, 3 below 1, 4 on the right, and 6 on the left. Cards 7 through 10 are laid to the side in a line, with card 7 on the bottom and card 10 on the top. (See diagram on page 30.)

1. The first card represents the present situation.
2. The second card represents the current challenges and blocks.
3. The third card represents the past and its influences.
4. The fourth card represents the immediate past, what you're moving from.
5. The fifth card represents what to focus on and the bigger picture for the future.
6. The sixth card represents a direction to take in the immediate future.
7. The seventh card explains the person's psyche and shows the attitude and behavioral patterns associated with such attitudes. Is it possible to look at your actions from the eyes of another and accept some things you need to change? What approach would be appropriate in this situation?

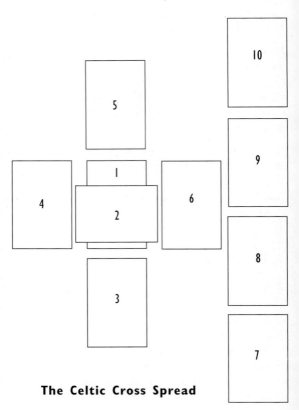

The Celtic Cross Spread

8. The eighth card is about environment and the energy within; energy being extremely important and sometimes difficult for more empathic people to process without the magical tools. Are the current situations, interactions, and environments having a negative or positive impact on the person's well-being? Is it time to rethink life?

9. The ninth card is a revelation card. It speaks to the person's hopes, desires, and fear; it reminds him or her to stay connected to one's intuition and to the current situation at hand. It helps a person to wake up to things of which one should be aware and that are having an influence on his or her behavior.

10. The tenth and final card explains if the person can avoid a possible future problem or if it is something for them to experience and learn from so as to evolve.

THE HORSESHOE SPREAD

This spread is a seven-card layout. There are three cards placed on each side of a center card in the shape of a horseshoe, which is read from left to right.

The first card represents the past. The second card represents the present. The third card represents hidden influences. The fourth card represents the person who is being read. The fifth card represents the attitudes of others the person finds themselves around. The sixth card represents what the person should do. The seventh card represents the outcome of possible actions.

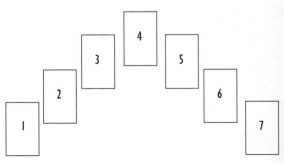

The Horseshoe Spread